SONS OF THUNDER
THE CARTOON SERIES FOR CHRISTIANS

STEPHEN PAUL GROW

Clay Bridges
PRESS

I0083001

Sons Of Thunder
The Cartoon Series For Christians
Copyright © 2023 by Stephen Grow
Illustrated by Stephen Grow

Published by Clay Bridges Press in Houston, TX
www.ClayBridgesPress.com

Scripture quotations marked (ESV) are taken from the ESV® Bible (The Holy Bible, English Standard Version®), copyright © 2001 by Crossway, a publishing ministry of Good News Publishers. Used by permission. All rights reserved.

ISBN: 978-1-68488-055-3
eISBN: 978-1-68488-056-0

Special Sales: Most Clay Bridges titles are available in special quantity discounts. Custom imprinting or excerpting can also be done to fit special needs. Contact Clay Bridges at Info@ClayBridgesPress.com

This book is dedicated to my wife, Mary Elizabeth Grow:
She has it all, she does it all, and she is gorgeous.
This book's for you!

⚡

In the beginning . . .
The idea for the title Sons of Thunder came from none other than Jesus himself. In Mark 3:17, when Jesus appointed the twelve apostles, he included two of Zebedee's sons, James and John, "to whom he gave the name Boanerges, that is, Sons of Thunder" (ESV). Jesus had an incredible sense of humor, and that inspired me to create a cartoon series using that name as its title. In 1993 and 1994 the series ran in a Christian biweekly newspaper under the title. Boanerges, which is Aramaic for "Sons of Thunder."

Phase two . . .
After Sons of Thunder had appeared in the newspaper, I had hopes to syndicate the series. As syndication didn't come intro fruition, I stored the original drawings in my basement in frustration, and there they sat for 28 years. In the summer of 2021, I was researching my family tree when I searched on the name of one of my ancestors. My search led me to Daniel who has become a very dear friend. We began our communications after I learned that we share my ancestor's last name; however, at this time we have not confirmed if we are in fact related (but we are still enjoying the research project in hopes that we might be distant cousins!)

In one of our many email conversations, the subject of cartoons came up, and I told him that I had published cartoons. He asked me to email him some of my cartoons. As I retrieved them from the storage box in my basement, the cloud of frustration and stress that once strained my view of them was lifted immediately. I felt blessed to have created this cartoon series; what's more, they looked and read awesome to me. When Daniel received the copies, he encouraged me to create more.

Out of gratitude and because he is my dear friend, I decided to write him into the new series as a recurring character. In real life, my friend Daniel is a police officer in Bavaria, Germany. As I started to illustrate him in his awesome uniform, I realized how cool it would be to feature a Bavarian police officer in the series. His character adds depth and intrigue to the cast of characters. Sons of Thunder is no longer solely an American cartoon; it has gone international; thanks to Daniel, it is a German-American series.

Zebedee

Zebedee is a purebred cartoon cat who specializes in sarcasm. He never talks to the other characters but bestows his wisdom on the reader. He hates all dogs but reserves a special disdain for Rottweilers. Zebedee loves to accompany the family to church softball games. He finds church softball appealing because he is amused by its silliness, and for Zebedee, human silliness is fuel for the sarcasm in his soul. According to him, softball is a game in which humans hit a ball that was intended to be missed. Then they run around a diamond and celebrate when they reach the last corner, which just happens to be the very corner they started from in the first place! Did I mention that he hates dogs? Although Zebedee thinks humans are silly, don't be caught mocking his human family in his presence. He would tumble with even a Rottweiler, if he heard one doing so!

James

James is 13 years old; he is the older brother of John. James finds himself in hot water with his parents more often than John does, but the two together are quite the comical challenge for their parents. James loves church softball and has a crush on a classmate named Chelsea. He often writes poems about her. He is torn between wanting to become the next greatest athlete or the next gospel superstar singer/songwriter. James desperately struggles with the French language and unfortunately for him, French is a school requirement. John is not only his brother, but he also doubles as James's best friend, but he would never tell John that.

John

John is 12 years old. He is more likely to be seen playing chess than a video game, but he plays both. John loves to play church softball. He likes to ask questions, and girls get on his nerves. He always outperforms James in school and lacks humility when discussing this topic with his older brother. His favorite Bible verse is, "Taking the five loaves and the two fish and looking up to heaven, he gave thanks and broke the loaves. Then he gave them to his disciples to distribute to the people along with softball trophies." Okay, he tweaked the Scripture! James is not only his brother, but he also doubles as John's best friend, but he would never tell James that.

Daniel is a Bavarian police officer. He may be a distant relative of Steve as his surname appears in Steve's family tree. While researching his ancestry, Steve found Daniel's email address and contacted him. Their ancestors originally lived near each other, which means that Daniel and Steve could be distant cousins. They developed a close relationship as a result of this connection. Daniel loves American football. He lives with his wonderful wife and daughter in Bavaria and longs for the day when Steve, Mary, the boys, and Zebedee can visit them. He has a great sense of humor and is extremely intelligent.

Daniel

Pastor Pete is more than the pastor at Steve and Mary's church; he is also a close friend of the entire family. He loves church softball and golf. He often finds himself inquiring about or correcting James and John's youthful, comical comments concerning Christianity and the Bible. When visiting the family, he jokes with Steve—when Zebedee is nearby—that he's thinking about getting a Rottweiler, followed by a wink and a nod. As a pastor who is not overly zealous about material possessions, he thoroughly enjoys his classic antique pickup truck.

Pastor Pete

Steve is the father of James and John and the husband of Mary. He is 34 years old and is a cartoonist. He and fellow character Daniel are best friends. Steve loves church softball and often golfs with his boys and Pastor Pete. He believes that Mary is out of his league, but often forgets to buy her flowers.

Steve

Mary is Steve's loving wife and mother of James and John. She is an instructional assistant at the boys' school. She loves church softball and often finds herself having to give her husband hints about becoming a better man, even though she doesn't otherwise enjoy repetition. She keeps the family unit on track in these challenging times, but Steve tries to claim equal credit by virtue of the fact that he chose her to be his wife. In the beginning when God said, "Let there be light," he could have used her smile to accomplish that task.

Mary

— SONS OF THUNDER —

— SONS OF THUNDER —

- SONS OF THUNDER -

- SONS OF THUNDER -

— SONS OF THUNDER —

- SONS OF THUNDER -

SAD BUT TRUE

DRUG STORIES HAVE SEVERAL PLOTS!

GROW © 1994

— SONS OF THUNDER —

James, want a peek at God's great universe? One moment... I think I just discovered a new Black Hole.
How can you see anything with the lens cap still on?
GROW ©2022
C
– SONS OF THUNDER –

— SONS OF THUNDER —

www.ingramcontent.com/pod-product-compliance
Lightning Source LLC
Chambersburg PA
CBHW060900090426
42737CB00026B/3499